100
BEST-SELLING
ALBUMS OF THE
90s

100
BEST-SELLING
ALBUMS OF THE

Dan Auty • Justin Cawthorne • Chris Barrett • Peter Dodd

THUNDER BAY
P · R · E · S · S
San Diego, California

Thunder Bay Press
An imprint of Printers Row Publishing Group
10350 Barnes Canyon Road, Suite 100, San Diego, CA 92121
www.thunderbaybooks.com

Copyright © 2018 Amber Books Ltd

All rights reserved. No part of this publication may be reproduced, distributed, or transmitted in any form or by any means, including photocopying, recording, or other electronic or mechanical methods, without the prior written permission of the publisher, except in the case of brief quotations embodied in critical reviews and certain other noncommercial uses permitted by copyright law.

Printers Row Publishing Group is a division of Readerlink Distribution Services, LLC. Thunder Bay Press is a registered trademark of Readerlink Distribution Services, LLC.

All notations of errors or omissions should be addressed to Thunder Bay Press, Editorial Department, at the above address.

All other correspondence (author inquiries, permissions) concerning the content of this book should be addressed to
Amber Books, United House, North Road, London, N7 9DP, United Kingdom
www.amberbooks.co.uk
Project Editor: Tom Broder
Design: Colin Hawes
Picture Research: Natasha Jones
Consultant: Roger Watson

Thunder Bay Press
Publisher: Peter Norton
Associate Publisher: Ana Parker
Publishing/Editorial Team: April Farr, Kelly Larsen, Kathryn C. Dalby
Editorial Team: JoAnn Padgett, Melinda Allman, Traci Douglas

Library of Congress Cataloging-in-Publication Data

Names: Auty, Dan, author. | Barrett, Chris (Music journalist) author. |
Cawthorne, Justin, author. | Dodd, Peter (Music journalist) author.
Title: 100 best-selling albums of the 90s / Dan Auty, Chris Barrett, Justin Cawthorne, and Peter Dodd.
Description: San Diego, CA : Thunder Bay Press, 2018. | Includes index.
Identifiers: LCCN 2017058758 (print) | LCCN 2017059185 (ebook) | ISBN 9781684125012 | ISBN 9781684123650 (paper over board)
Subjects: LCSH: Popular music--1991-2000--Discography.
Classification: LCC ML156.4.P6 (ebook) | LCC ML156.4.P6 A96 2018 (print) | DDC 016.78164026/6--dc23
LC record available at https://lccn.loc.gov/2017058758

Printed in China

22 21 20 19 18   2 3 4 5 6

Contents

Editor's Foreword

The ranking of the 100 best-selling albums of the 1990s listed in the following pages is based upon the number of platinum and multi-platinum sales awards each album has achieved, as certified by the Recording Industry Association of America (RIAA) and the British Phonographic Industry (BPI). The RIAA platinum award represents sales of at least one million albums; the BPI platinum award represents sales of at least 300,000 albums.

In an industry not always noted for the accuracy of its published figures, these awards provide one of the most reliable measures of sales success. Unlike lists based on chart position, these figures show sales from the date of first release right up to the present day. This means that an album such as No Doubt's *Tragic Kingdom*, which failed to chart on release in 1995 but has sold well ever since, is rated above Vanilla Ice's *To the Extreme*, which spent 16 weeks at Number One but could not maintain these sales for any length of time.

Ranking of equal sellers

Where two or more albums in the list have the same sales total they are arranged by date of release, with the more recent album ranked highest, since its sales are stronger relative to time spent on the market. U2's 1991 album *Achtung Baby*, for example, has had almost seven more years to achieve sales of 9,500,000 than Lauryn Hill's 1998 release *The Miseducation of Lauryn Hill*, and is therefore ranked lower in the list.

Compilations and soundtracks

Compilation or greatest hits albums are not included in this list, although live albums and original movie or musical soundtracks, where all of the songs have been collected together or recorded specifically for the album, are featured. The soundtrack to the 1994 film *Forrest Gump*, for example, featured tracks from artists ranging from Elvis and Joan Baez to The Supremes, and helped introduce a whole new generation to classic songs from the preceding decades.

US and international album sales

Although the lists in this book are based on both US and UK album sales, the sheer size of the North American album market relative to that of other regions means that the list is inevitably weighted toward US top-sellers. Nonetheless, British acts are well represented, with albums from artists ranging from Eric Clapton and Oasis to the Spice Girls all featuring.

The albums are illustrated with a mixture of US and UK sleeve designs—a selection that includes some of the most iconic cover images of the decade.

Facts and figures

The appendices provide a breakdown of some of the most interesting facts and figures from the book. You can find out which artists have the most albums in the list and who are the highest-ranking US and UK acts. You can see which albums have won the most Grammy Awards or contain the most Number One singles, what are the best-selling soundtracks and live albums, and which record labels were the most successful of the decade.

Alongside entries from old favorites there are enough surprises to keep the most dedicated music buff guessing: Nirvana's genre-defining 1991 album *Nevermind*, for example, was comfortably outsold by fellow grunge-rockers Pearl Jam's album *Ten*, released just a few months earlier, while the Cranberries outsold Sheryl Crow, Will Smith outsold Michael Jackson, and Jewel outsold Mariah Carey.

Carlos Santana's 1999 release
Supernatural, his 28th album in a
career spanning four decades,
won eight Grammy Awards, more
than any other album featured in the
100 best-selling albums of the 1990s.

The Best-selling Albums of the 1990s

In the 1990s, the album charts opened up to encompass a greater variety of sounds and styles than ever before. Grunge bands like Pearl Jam and Nirvana brought guitar rock and a punk aesthetic back into the mainstream. Hip-hop finally began to reap the commercial rewards that it had promised for so long, silencing those who had dismissed it as a fad, and other urban sounds, from R&B to dance, filled the charts. There was room, too, for strong, commercial pop. But it was country music that really dominated the decade, with artists such as Garth Brooks and Shania Twain helping reinvigorate the genre, injecting it with a healthy dose of sex and style.

The decade saw women become market leaders in a way that exceeded even Madonna's achievements in the 1980s. Not many people would have bet that the end of the decade would see a female country singer at the top of the best-sellers, triumphantly tossing her cowboy hat in the air. But while Shania Twain led the pack, she was not the only female artist to ride high in the charts. Female solo artists, from Alanis Morissette to Melissa Etheridge, dominated 1990s music, while girl bands such as TLC and the Spice Girls also gave the boys a good run for their money.

Fighting the pirates

The early 1990s saw the music industry enjoying a boom period. By 1992, sales of compact discs had outpaced cassette tapes and were growing all the time; the CD's unrivaled sound quality and ease of use made it the format of choice for most 1990s music buyers.

But there was a downside to the CD revolution—music pirates were quick to spot the potential for selling counterfeit CDs, adding an element of instability to the economics of the music industry. East Asia proved to be a haven for CD pirates; in the Philippines, the situation was so bad that it was estimated that half of all CDs sold there were pirate copies. The problem was by no means exclusive to Asia, however. In any European or North American city, traders could be found selling their wares on street corners. By the end of the 1990s, it was estimated that more than 640 million pirated discs were sold annually.

Technological advances

Illegal CDs were not the only problem facing the music industry. The creation in 1997 of the MP3—a digital file format that allowed audio files to be reduced in size and transmitted over the Internet—meant that anyone with an MP3 player or a CD writer could download and record music illegally. Several major courtroom battles between record companies and illicit net operators did little to contain the problem, although the full effects of the new technology on the album market would not be felt until after the end of the decade.

The 1990s also saw a growing number of bands embracing the opportunities offered by the Internet, by giving concerts on the net or providing fans with the opportunity to legally download music clips. Hootie & the Blowfish, one of the more bizarrely named bands to grace the charts, played an Internet concert from Chicago's House of Blues in October 1998. Their 1994 album *Cracked Rear View* had sold more than 10 million copies by the winter of 1995, making it Atlantic Records' best-seller.

Established artists
The 1990s album chart also featured plenty of old-timers rubbing shoulders with fresh new talent like Hootie. CDs and the Internet were unheard of when Carlos Santana formed his band Santana in the 1960s. Three decades later, Santana were back at the top of the album chart with *Supernatural*, an album featuring

The angst-filled songs on Alanis Morissette's multi-platinum album *Jagged Little Pill*—like the harder, punk-inspired sound of grunge bands such as Nirvana— showed that in the 1990s, "angry" definitely sold records.

collaborations with a host of 1990s stars including Lauryn Hill and Eagle-Eye Cherry. In December 1996, Carlos Santana received a prestigious Century Award from *Billboard* magazine, honoring his contribution to music.

Meat Loaf was another established star who continued to do good business in the 1990s. His gothic rock-opera masterpiece *Bat Out of Hell* was originally released in 1977, when it had even managed to knock *Saturday Night Fever* off the top of the Australian chart. The sequel, *Bat Out of Hell II*, was released 16 years later in 1993, when it made the Number One spot on both sides of the Atlantic. Another seasoned performer was Eric Clapton, who did particularly well with *Unplugged*, recorded during his acoustic concert for MTV in January 1992.

Cowgirls and cowboys

Shania Twain led a growing band of 1990s artists who fused country with pop and rock, taking country music away from its large but middle-aged specialist audience and widening its appeal. Released in November 1997, Twain's mega-selling album *Come on Over* showed the level of this appeal by topping the country and mainstream charts simultaneously. Twain's songwriting and production partner was her then-husband, the heavy metal producer "Mutt"

Lange, who had powered Def Leppard to fame.

Hot on Twain's trail came the Dixie Chicks, three cowgirl divas who crossed barriers with their dramatic album *Wide Open Spaces* to become the best-selling country act in 1998. Garth Brooks also rode tall with two Top 20 studio albums and a Top 20 live album in the 1990s album charts. Like Shania Twain, Brooks redefined country, producing haunting, mystical songs that soon had other artists lining up to cover them. According to figures from the Recording Industry Association of America (RIAA), Brooks has sold more than 148 million albums—12 million more than Elvis Presley.

Even Whitney Houston was influenced by country music in the 1990s. The soundtrack album to her movie *The Bodyguard* featured a revamp of Dolly Parton's country classic "I Will Always Love You." Houston's big-production power ballad spent a record-breaking 14 weeks at the top of the US singles chart.

Girl power

Alanis Morissette was no newcomer to fame in the 1990s. As a child she had featured on the TV cable show *You Can't Do That On Television*; further acting roles as she grew up helped her finance her early recording career. By the 1990s, though, she had grown into an uncompromising and tough singer-songwriter. Morissette's 1995 album, *Jagged Little Pill*, was a million miles away from fellow starlet Britney Spears' bubblegum pop image, and won the Canadian two Grammy Awards. The decade also saw the emergence of Sheryl Crow, an outspoken singer-songwriter. One retail outlet even stopped selling Crow's records when she had the gall to criticize their policies, but her albums flew off the shelves elsewhere. By 1997, her sales had reached triple-platinum status.

The decade also proved a rewarding one for Bonnie Raitt. Her album *Nick of Time* hit Number One on the US album chart in spring 1990 and was followed in 1991 with the Grammy-winning *Luck of the Draw*. Raitt's recording career dated back to the 1970s, and in many ways she could consider herself to be the musical godmother of both Alanis Morissette and Sheryl Crow.

Other female artists chose to tread safer territories. Celine Dion's *Titanic* love theme "My Heart Will Go On" was a classic pop epic, melting the iciest heart. The song helped turn the *Titanic* soundtrack and Dion's own album *Let's Talk About Love* into multi-platinum best-sellers.

Boy bands

The 1990s also had its fair share of boy bands. The decade's pre-eminent example, the

Female solo artists dominated the 1990s album market, but the Dixie Chicks' Grammy-winning album, *Wide Open Spaces*, showed that girl bands could top the charts too.

Backstreet Boys, were named after Backstreet Market, a shopping area in Orlando, Florida. Legend has it that the Backstreet Boys landed a major recording deal after their co-manager, Donna Wright, phoned a Jive Records executive on her cellphone from one of their early concerts. The executive heard the screaming crowd and the band was signed up the very next day.

The decade saw a plethora of former television child stars grow up and turn into hot chart material. Two members of *N Sync, the 1990s other chart-topping boy band, had cut their teeth working on the Disney Channel's *Mickey Mouse Club*, as had Britney Spears. Spears and *N Sync's Justin Timberlake later started dating, and the antics of the two young pop icons fueled the gossip columns for years.

Brit pop

In the UK, the Spice Girls were formed as the answer to British boy bands such as Take That and belted out a fistful of punchy songs, attracting worldwide interest. But anyone who expected a return to the days when British music dominated the charts would be disappointed. On an international scale, the Brit-pop boom of the mid-1990s created ripples rather than tidal waves, and many British artists found it difficult to reach out across the Atlantic. One of the great exceptions to this was Oasis. In 1994, the group won the best UK band category in the MTV European Music Awards and in 1996 their album *(What's the Story) Morning Glory?* slid into the US album chart at Number Four. Unashamedly influenced by Lennon and McCartney, Oasis were hailed by some as the new Beatles, although many found their style derivative.

Another British band to achieve significant US success was UK grunge-rockers Bush, although, intriguingly, the band were never accepted to quite the same extent in their homeland. Meanwhile, Irish rock superstars U2 continued to receive critical acclaim, exploring dark themes with their ambitious 1991 album *Achtung Baby*, and Irish quartet the Cranberries charted strongly with 1994's *No Need To Argue*.

Rockers and grungers

America had never really taken to punk, but kids in the 1990s were more than willing to embrace punk's more accessible offspring—grunge. The grunge-rock movement grew as a reaction to the surplus of complacent, well-groomed talent in the album chart. Suddenly, it was cool to upset your parents again.

The prime exponents of this music, such as godfathers of grunge Pearl Jam and Nirvana, came from Seattle. Pearl Jam's album, *Ten*, was close to selling 10 million copies by August 1992, and Nirvana could boast similar sales with *Nevermind*. Tracks such as "Smells Like Teen Spirit" and "Come As You Are" from *Nevermind* became grunge anthems, with sales further fueled by Kurt Cobain's suicide by shotgun in April 1994.

Meanwhile, the 1980s stadium-rock bands such as Bon Jovi and Def Leppard were increasingly sidelined by the new heavy metal movement represented by bands like Metallica. Some of Metallica's shows were more like battlefields than concerts. In a March 1992 concert in Florida, Metallica fans dangled a security guard by his ankles from the balcony. Four months later, Metallica guitarist and vocalist James Hetfield was rushed to the hospital suffering from serious burns after a stage effect exploded during a concert in Montreal. Hetfield recovered, although accidents and controversy continued to follow the band. Nonetheless, Metallica's album sales remained huge. In 1999, the RIAA gave them a diamond award for selling more than 10 million copies of their album, *Metallica*.

Nirvana's 1991 album *Nevermind* turned frontman Kurt Cobain into a major rock icon and paved the way for the explosion of grunge bands in the mid-1990s.

Rap and R&B

The 1990s saw fresh developments in rap music, hip-hop, and R&B that would feed the record industry for many years to come. The first moves were made by Vanilla Ice and MC Hammer, whose album, *Please Hammer, Don't Hurt 'Em,* was recorded for a lowly $10,000 but spent 21 weeks at the top of the album chart. Advertisers were quick to pick up on the marketing potential offered by dance music. MC Hammer signed a deal with British Knights athletic footwear and Pepsi-Cola. Several other artists also signed lucrative sponsorship deals.

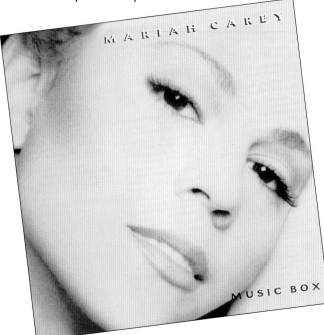

The huge success of albums such as *Music Box* made Mariah Carey the decade's pre-eminent R&B star.

Bad boys

Although hip-hop and R&B became increasingly bankable, the music had more than its fair share of trouble in the 1990s. Among other incidents, Whitney Houston's husband Bobby Brown faced drug and assault charges, Boyz II Men's tour manager was shot dead in Chicago, and R. Kelly had to cancel a concert when he and his entourage were involved in a brawl.

The gangsta-rap movement of the late 1980s played out to its logical conclusion in 1996–97 with the violent deaths of two of hip-hop's biggest stars, Tupac Shakur and the Notorious B.I.G. Their deaths did little to dent the music's popularity. The Notorious B.I.G's murder most likely helped push sales of his posthumously released *Life After Death* over the 10 million mark and inspired Puff Daddy's "I'll Be Missing You."

But 1990s hip-hop and R&B had much more to offer than gangstas and drive-by shootings. The Fugees' debut album, *The Score*, provided a welcome antidote to the macho posturing of other rappers, and their version of Roberta Flack's 1973 hit "Killing Me Softly" became a classic lovers' anthem. *The Score* was named R&B Album of the Year at the 1996 *Billboard* Music Awards. Will Smith, meanwhile, proved that hip-hop didn't have to rely on violence or profanity to appeal to record buyers.

Mariah Carey, with her impish looks and five-octave range, became the best-selling R&B diva of the 1990s. Her three biggest albums of the decade sold more than 31 million copies between them. Meanwhile, R&B boy band Boyz II Men formed at Philadelphia's High School of Creative and Performing Arts, where their tight harmony style quickly gained them plenty of attention. Like Whitney Houston, Boyz II Men contributed to a couple of big movie hits—"End of the Road" was featured in the Eddie Murphy movie *Boomerang* and "I Will Get There" was used on the soundtrack to *The Prince of Egypt*.

Innovation and diversity

The 1990s began with some commentators wondering whether the growing popularity of computer games would stop kids from spending money on music; the decade ended with many in the industry expressing concerns about the effects of illegal downloading on record sales. In fact, 1990s music was anything but in a crisis— the album charts show an industry in fine health, both in terms of the profits and the quality and diversity of music available. The great virtue of 1990s music was that it never settled into a niche or grew complacent, but continued to innovate, bringing new and different styles and sounds into the mainstream.

The Miseducation of Lauryn Hill, a fluid blend of hip-hop, soul, and R&B, won Hill five Grammy Awards (and six more nominations) to add to the two Grammy Awards she had picked up with The Fugees for their 1996 album The Score.

100 Yes I Am

| • **Album sales:** 6,150,000 | • **Release date:** September 1993 |

Her fourth release, *Yes I Am* was Melissa Etheridge's breakthrough album and commercially her most successful. The title was widely taken to signal the singer publicly acknowledging her homosexuality for the first time. The sound was a powerful collection of anthemic blues rock, distinguished by her deep, rasping vocals and heartfelt lyrics.

Etheridge plays with the same group of musicians throughout—including prolific session guitarman Waddy Wachtel and ex-Small Face Ian McLagan—helping to give the album a concise, consistent tone. Producer Hugh Padgham, who had worked extensively with Phil Collins and Sting, brought the same dynamic, commercial sense to this album. The opening track, "I'm the Only One," is a defiant, churning rocker and sets the tone. "'If I Wanted To," "All American Girl," and "Resist" rock out in a similar style. Etheridge shows her subtler, more emotional side in tracks like the acoustic-based "Come To My Window" and "I Will Never Be the Same."

Yes I Am reached Number 15 on the *Billboard* Top 200 and produced two Top 30 singles—"I'm the Only One" and "Come To My Window." Both were nominated for Best Rock Song at the 1995 Grammy Awards, at which Etheridge won the award for Best Female Vocal Rock Performance.

Number One singles:
None

Grammy Awards: Best Female Rock Vocal Performance: "Come To My Window"

Label: US: Polygram; UK: Island

Recorded in:
Los Angeles, USA

Personnel:
Melissa Etheridge
Waddy Wachtel
James Fearnley
Ian McLagan
Scott Thurston
Pino Palladino
Kevin McCormick
David Sutton
Mauricio Fritz Lewak

Producer:
Hugh Padgham

1. I'm the Only One (4:54)
2. If I Wanted To (3:55)
3. Come To My Window (3:55)
4. Silent Legacy (5:22)
5. I Will Never Be the Same (4:41)
6. All American Girl (4:05)
7. Yes I Am (4:24)
8. Resist (2:57)
9. Ruins (4:53)
10. Talking To My Angel (4:48)

Total album length: 44 minutes

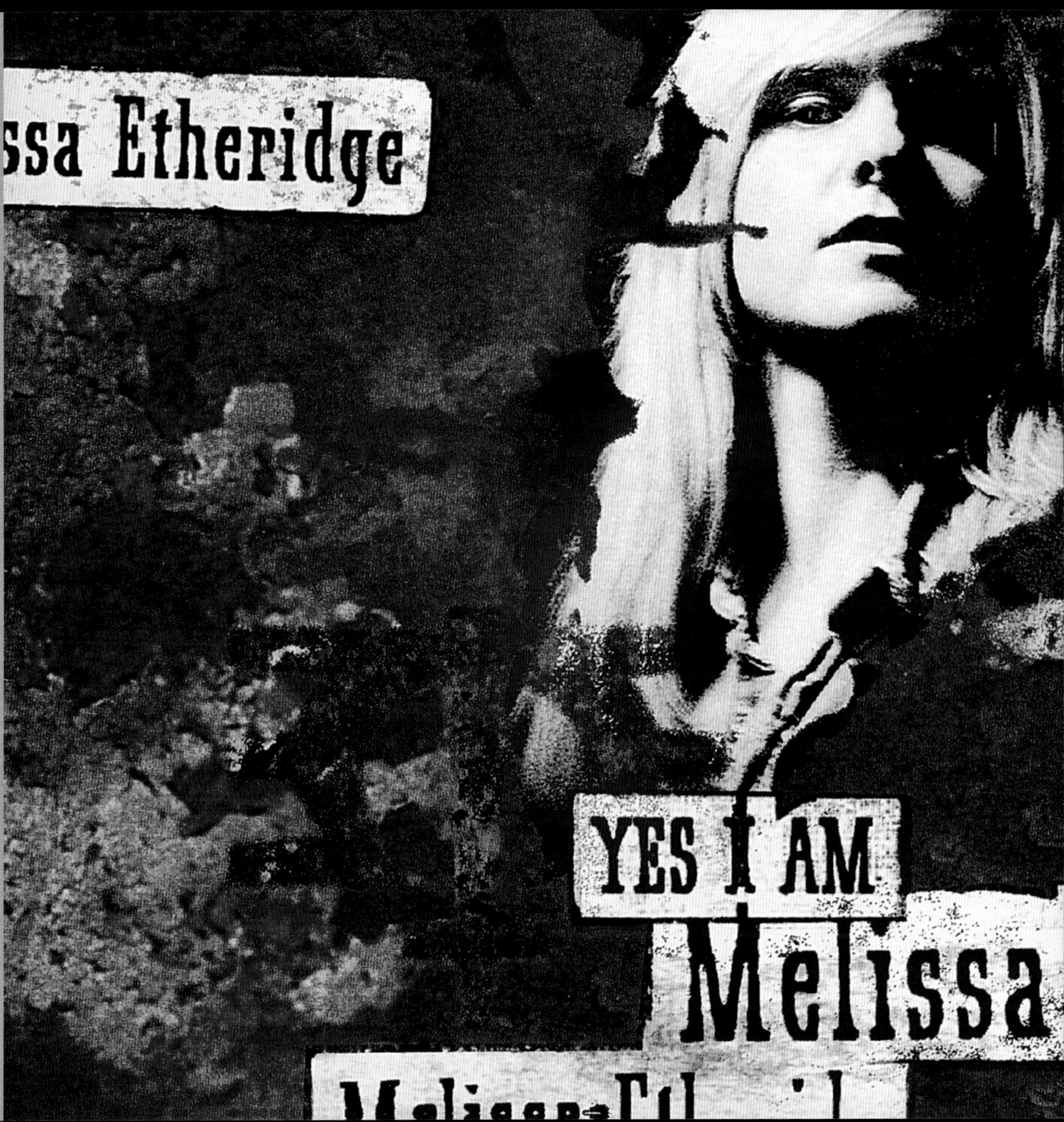
ssa Etheridge
YES I AM
Melissa

Four

The band's fourth album, the appropriately titled *Four*, was a major breakthrough for Blues Traveler. Although the blues band had developed its skills and reputation through years of touring with their harmonica-infused blues-rock gaining fans, it wasn't until their 1995 single "Run-Around" that they launched into mainstream recognition. The song became one of the biggest singles of the year. With nearly 12 months on the charts, the single is now unofficially the longest-serving record on the US charts.

The sleeve image for the album came about after an incident early in Blues Traveler's career. Following a recorded rehearsal in New Jersey, the band was joined by a black cat while listening to the tape. Once the music ended the cat departed, inspiring the band to adopt the attentive feline's image as their long-running mascot, and eventually hiring an artist friend to design the album cover.

The album's closing track, "Brother John," was written by the late bassist Bobby Sheehan about his younger brother, whose personal problems foreshadowed Bobby's own drug overdose in August 1999.

Two years after its release, *Four* was still on the US charts, having amassed more than four million sales. The album managed to reach Number Eight in the US, but failed to chart in the UK.

Number One singles:
None

Grammy Awards: Best Rock Performance by a Duo or Group With Vocal

Label: US: A&M; UK: Polydor

Recorded in: Woodstock, USA

Personnel:
John Popper
Chan Kinchla
Bobby Sheehan
Brendan Hill
Jono Manson
Warren Haynes
Peter Malcolm Kavakavich
Chuck Leavell
Paul Shaffer
Bashiri Johnson

Producers:
Steve Thompson
Michael Barbiero

1. Run-Around (4:40)
2. Stand (5:19)
3. Look Around (5:42)
4. Fallible (4:47)
5. The Mountains Win Again (5:06)
6. Freedom (4:01)
7. Crash Burn (2:59)
8. Price to Pay (5:17)
9. Hook (4:49)
10. The Good, the Bad, and the Ugly (1:55)
11. Just Wait (5:34)
12. Brother John (6:38)

Total album length: 57 minutes

BLUES TRAVELER

four

98 Blue

| • **Album sales:** 6,150,000 | • **Release date:** July 1996 |

A combination of canny PR and natural talent made LeAnn Rimes a country star while just a teenager. Promoter Bill Mack had discovered Rimes when she was only 11 and earmarked a song he had written during the 1960s, "Blue," as the perfect showcase for her talents. Mack's story was that he had written "Blue" for Patsy Cline, but the country legend had died before recording it. Since then he had been waiting for Cline's successor to come along. While the press absorbed the story wholesale, the truth was that the song had been recorded by three different artists since the 1960s. Still, "Blue" proved the perfect choice to launch Rimes' career and establish her as a major country star.

The song broke a new record for a country music single, selling more than 100,000 copies during its first week on release. It earned Rimes two Grammys and a nomination for Country Music Association Best Country Singer, making Rimes the youngest artist ever to receive a CMA nomination. *Blue* reached Number Three on the *Billboard* Top 200.

Number One singles:
None

Grammy Awards:
Best New Artist; Best Female Country Vocal Performance: "Blue"

Label: US & UK: Curb

Recorded in: Clovis & Nashville, USA

Personnel:
LeAnn Rimes
Eddy Arnold
Johnny Mulhair
Jerry Matheny
M. Spriggs
Dan Huff
Brent Rowan
John Jorgenson
Milo Deering
Bruce Bouton
Paul Franklin
Larry Franklin
Kevin Bailey
Paul Goad
Jimmy Kelly
Mike McLain
John Hobbs
Steve Nathan
Kelly Glenn
Curtis Randel
Mike Chapman
Glenn Worf
Bob Smith
Fred Gleber
Brad Billingsley
Greg Morrow
Chad Cromwell
Terry McMillan
Joy McKay
Perry Coleman
Mary Ann Kennedy
Various other personnel

Producers:
Wilbur C. Rimes
Chuck Howard

1. Blue (2:47)
2. Hurt Me (2:53)
3. One Way Ticket (Because I Can) (3:52)
4. My Baby (2:49)
5. Honestly (3:21)
6. The Light in Your Eyes (3:20)
7. Talk to Me (3:11)
8. I'll Get Even With You (3:18)
9. Cattle Call (3:07)
10. Good Lookin' Man (3:11)
11. Fade to Blue (3:03)

Total album length: 34 minutes

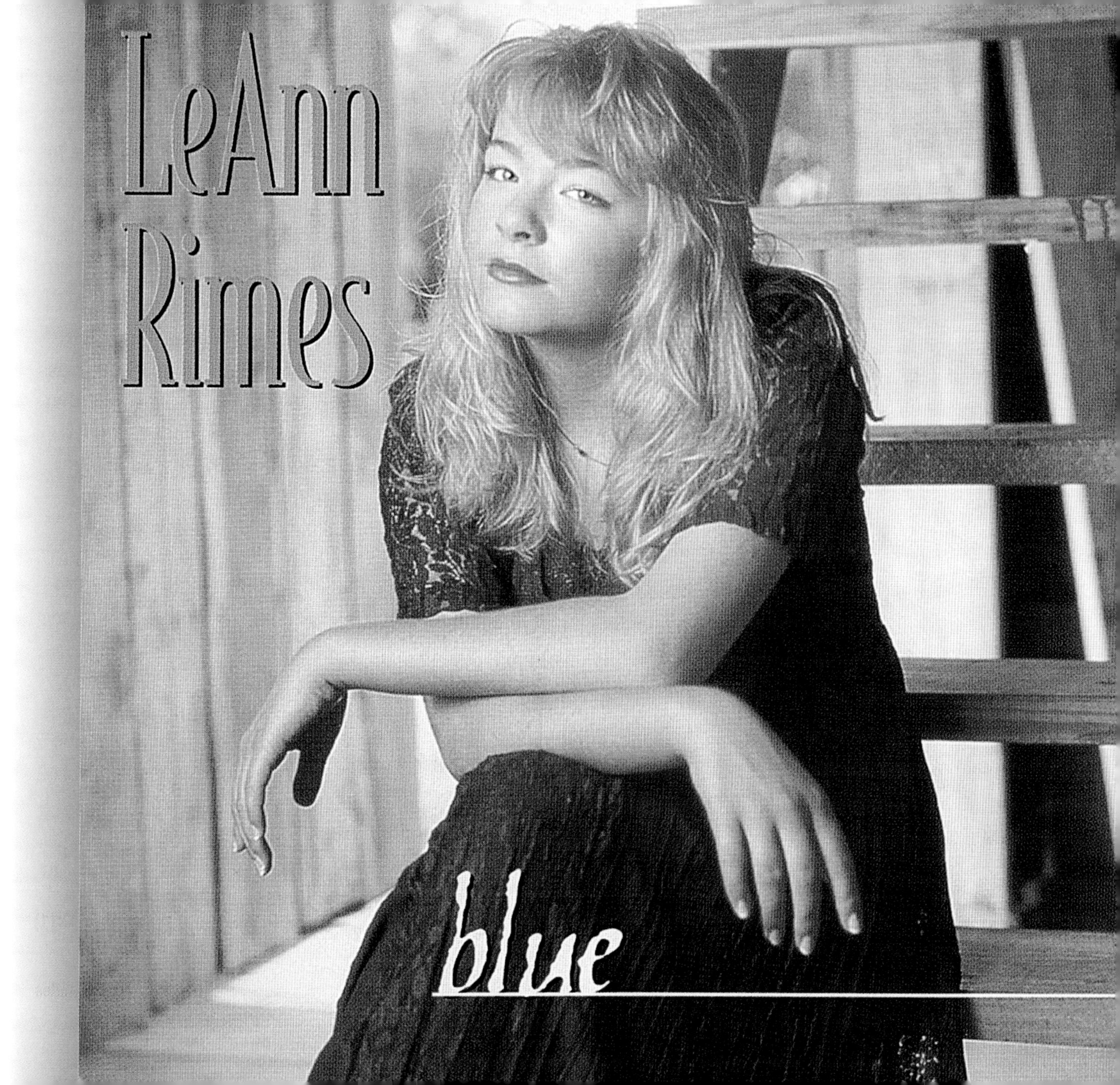
LeAnn
Rimes
blue

97 Space Jam

| • **Album sales:** 6,150,000 | • **Release date:** November 1996 |

The soundtrack to *Space Jam*—the live-action/animation movie featuring basketball star Michael Jordan and a host of Looney Tunes characters—represents the modern trend for broadening a movie's appeal through careful marketing of the album. Indeed, a number of tracks featured in the movie don't even make it onto the album, which instead favors a more marketable mix of gentle R&B, light hip-hop, and straightforward pop.

The album was just one part of a huge media-wide *Space Jam* event. Warner tied in the launch of a new toy division and the opening of the New York Warner Brothers store to the release of the movie and album. Powered by R. Kelly's smash hit "I Believe I Can Fly," the *Space Jam* soundtrack reached Number Two in the US and peaked at Number Five in the UK.

Number One singles:
None

Grammy Awards: Best Male R&B Performance; Best R&B Song; Best Song Written for a Motion Picture or for Television: "I Believe I Can Fly"

Label: US & UK: Atlantic

Recorded in:
Various locations

Personnel:
Chris Rock
Seal
Barry White
David Foster
Coolio
R. Kelly
Biz Markie

Busta Rhymes
LL Cool J
Method Man
D'Angelo
Monica
Robin S
Various other personnel

Producers:
Seal
Brian Dobbs
Jay McGowan
C.C. Lemonhead
David Foster
Rashad Smith
Armando Colon
Todd Terry
Lou Adler
Jamey Jaz
Jimmy Jam
Terry Lewis
R. Kelly
Various other producers

1. **Fly Like an Eagle (Seal) (4:14)**
2. **Winner (Coolio) (4:03)**
3. **Space Jam (Quad City DJs) (5:07)**
4. **I Believe I Can Fly (R Kelly) (5:22)**
5. **Hit 'Em High (B Real) (4:17)**
6. **I Found My Smile Again (D'Angelo) (6:15)**
7. **For You I Will (Monica) (4:56)**
8. **Upside Down (Salt-N-Pepa) (4:16)**
9. **Givin' U All That I've Got (Robin S) (4:04)**
10. **Basketball Jones (Chris Rock) (5:40)**
11. **I Turn to You (All-4-One) (4:52)**
12. **All of My Days (Changing Faces) (4:01)**
13. **That's the Way (I Like It) (Biz Markie) (3:49)**
14. **Buggin' (Billy West) (4:14)**

Total album length: 65 minutes

MUSIC FROM AND INSPIRED BY THE MOTION PICTURE

Third Eye Blind

| • **Album sales:** 6,200,000 | • **Release date:** April 1997 |

A bidding war erupted around the as yet unsigned Third Eye Blind prior to the release of their debut album. This was fueled mainly by frontman Stephan Jenkins' producing skills (as evidenced on The Braids' cover version of "Bohemian Rhapsody") and an impressive 1996 live performance opening for Oasis.

The group ultimately went with Elektra, whose CEO, Sylvia Rhodes, had actively demonstrated her support. The label proved willing not only to allow Jenkins to produce the debut album, but also signed him to help nurture other new bands.

Jenkins credits the four years it took to gain a contract as a contributing factor to the strength of the band's debut album. Of the 14 songs that were recorded, many originated from a 14-track demo that the group had used to gain attention. Engineer Eric Valentine, who had also helped produce the group's demos, was retained for the album. The final lineup was rehearsed in a San Francisco warehouse before being taken into the studio.

Ironically, the band's name and reputation were made with the single that least represented the album: "Semi-Charmed Life" became an MTV favorite despite the subject matter concerning addiction to speed. *Third Eye Blind* reached Number 25 on the *Billboard* Top 200.

Number One singles:
None

Grammy Awards: None

Label: US & UK: Elektra

Recorded in:
California, USA

Personnel:
Stephan Jenkins
Kevin Cadogan
Arion Salazar
Brad Hargreaves
Eric Valentine
Ari Gorman
Michael Urbano

Producers:
Ren Klyce
Eric Valentine
Stephan Jenkins
Kevin Cadogan

1. Losing a Whole Year (3:20)
2. Narcolepsy (3:48)
3. Semi-Charmed Life (4:28)
4. Jumper (4:32)
5. Graduate (3:09)
6. How's It Going To Be (4:13)
7. Thanks a Lot (4:57)
8. Burning Man (2:59)
9. Good For You (3:52)
10. London (3:07)
11. I Want You (4:29)
12. The Background (4:56)
13. Motorcycle Drive By (4:22)
14. God of Wine (5:17)

Total album length: 57 minutes

THIRD EYE BLIND

Dónde Jugarán Los Niños?

| • **Album sales:** 6,250,000 | • **Release date:** April 1994 |

Despite their Mexican roots, Maná owe a greater debt to straightforward pop-rock than the Latin rhythms of artists such as Ricky Martin. The band's unique sound and slick production values helped them to develop a passionate Latin American following several years before mainstream success beckoned. This popularity, and Mexico's thriving tourist industry, helped Maná achieve crossover success.

Dónde Jugarán Los Niños?, the band's second album, offered both catchy tunes and lyrics with a political message. While singer Fher's western-styled vocals—drawing frequent comparison to Sting—provide one of Maná's main hooks, vocal duties are shared here, as on other albums, with drummer Alex González. The title track translates as "Where Will the Children Play?" and reflects the social conscience that underscores the band's music as strongly as their sense of rhythm. The track serves as a plea not to ruin the Earth for future generations.

The album's success was in part fueled by the band's vivid concerts, which had resulted in a surge in popularity as the 1980s drew to a close. *Dónde Jugarán Los Niños?* spent 97 consecutive weeks in *Billboard*'s Latin Top 50, peaking at Number Four, and is regarded by many as the group's defining album.

Number One singles:
None

Grammy Awards: None

Label: US & UK: WEA

Recorded in:
Los Angeles, USA

Personnel:
Fher
Vampiro
Iván González
Juan Calleros
Alex González
Ramon Flores
Jose Quintana
Luis Conte
Sheila Rios

Producers:
Fher
Alex González
Jose Quintana

1. De Pies a Cabeza (4:35)
2. Oye Mi Amor (4:32)
3. Cachito (4:46)
4. Vivir Sin Aire (4:51)
5. Dónde Jugarán los Niños? (4:14)
6. El Desierto (4:09)
7. La Chula (4:07)
8. Como Te Deseo (4:30)
9. Te Lloré Un Rio (4:52)
10. Como Diablos (3:53)
11. Huele A Tristeza (4:43)
12. Me Vale (4:32)
13. Como Te Deseo [Remix Version] (4:43)
14. La Chula [Remix Version] (5:53)

Total album length: 64 minutes

2 VERSIONES EXTRA
EDICION ESPECIAL
INCLUYE LIBRO DE CANCIONES

MANA

donde jugarán los niños?

94 Purple

| • **Album sales:** 6,250,000 | • **Release date:** May 1994 |

After enduring criticism for their debut album, *Core*, which many felt owed a few too many debts to other grunge pioneers, Stone Temple Pilots made a conscious effort to distinguish themselves with *Purple*. The vilification continued, but *Purple* still debuted at Number One on the *Billboard* chart, and remained there for three weeks. In the UK, the album reached the Number 10 spot.

Under the guidance of producer Brendan O'Brien, Stone Temple Pilots managed to record and mix *Purple* in the space of three weeks. They had spent a year and a half touring *Core*, and had used the soundchecks to work on new material. By the time the group hit the studio again, they had somewhere in the region of 40 new songs to pick from. Partially escaping their grunge background, the group forged ahead with a harder rock sound, mixing strong riffs while never shying away from occasional acoustic moments. Cuts such as "Big Empty" and "Interstate Love Song" are considered to be among the band's finest work. *Purple* includes a hidden 12th track, "12 Gracious Melodies."

The commercial success of *Purple,* and the freedom it granted for the group to take a break, would take its toll, with singer Scott Weiland developing a heroin addiction in the years following the album's release. Weiland died of an accidental drug overdose while on tour in 2015.

Number One singles:
None

Grammy Awards: None

Label: US & UK: Atlantic

Recorded in: Minneapolis, USA

Personnel:
Scott Weiland
Dean DeLeo
Robert DeLeo
Eric Kretz
Paul Leary
Brendan O'Brien

Producer:
Brendan O'Brien

1. Meat Plow (3:37)
2. Vasoline (2:56)
3. Lounge Fly (5:18)
4. Interstate Love Song (3:14)
5. Still Remains (3:33)
6. Pretty Penny (3:42)
7. Silver Gun Superman (5:16)
8. Big Empty (4:54)
9. Unglued (2:34)
10. Army Ants (3:46)
11. Kitchen Ware & Candy Bars (8:06)

Total album length: 47 minutes

93 My Own Prison

| • **Album sales:** 6,250,000 | • **Release date:** June 1997 |

Creed's debut album, *My Own Prison*, was originally recorded for less than $6000, but took less than two years to reach triple-platinum status. Initially released independently, the album was remixed (by Soundgarden producer Ron Saint-Germain, who introduced a heavier, more radio-friendly sound) and re-released by Wind-Up Records six months later.

Frontman Scott Stapp had been raised in a strictly religious household in which rock music was forbidden. After he left home, he wrote most of the lyrics for *My Own Prison* in his car, which doubled as his temporary home. Ultimately, Stapp's religious background found its way into the songs, the subject matter of which tended toward both spiritual and social concerns, although never at the expense of Creed's straightforward, post-grunge rock sound.

Although the album peaked at Number 22 on the *Billboard* Top 200, sales of *My Own Prison* remained very strong with the release of four successful singles ("My Own Prison," "Torn," "What's This Life For," and "One") pushing the album on to greater heights. Despite the band receiving relatively little support from MTV or the mainstream media, this failed to impact on album sales, with more than five million copies of *My Own Prison* selling before the decade was up.

Number One singles:
None

Grammy Awards: None

Label: US: Wind-Up;
UK: Epic

Recorded in: Tallahassee
& Miami, USA

Personnel:
Mark Tremonti
Scott Stapp
Brian Marshall
Scott Phillips
John Kurzweg

Producer:
John Kurzweg

1. Torn (6:23)
2. Ode (4:57)
3. My Own Prison (4:58)
4. Pity For Dime (5:29)
5. In America (4:58)
6 Illusion (4:37)
7. Unforgiven (3:38)
8. Sister (4:56)
9. What's This Life For (4:08)
10. One (5:02)

Total album length: 54 minutes

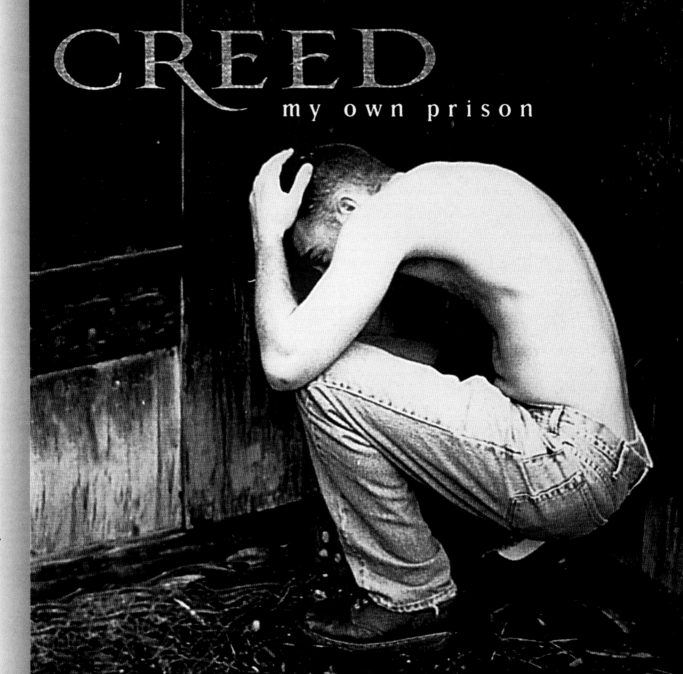

CREED
my own prison

Sleeve artwork by Justin Hobart Brown

Pure Country

| • **Album sales:** 6,300,000 | • **Release date:** September 1992 |

The early 1990s were a watershed for country music, the huge success of Garth Brooks signaling the emergence of a new generation of country stars. George Strait's more traditional brand of Texan swing—straight, no-frills country music—had little of Brooks's hype or arena-rock tendencies, yet he was one of the few country stars of the 1980s who continued to sell just as strongly throughout the 1990s.

The album *Pure Country* was a soundtrack to a movie that starred Strait as a disillusioned country superstar who retreats to his roots in the heartlands of America. The movie won Strait the Tex Ritter Award at the Academy of Country Music (ACM) awards. The music is an enticing mix of sentimental, fiddle-laden ballads such as "When Did You Stop Loving Me" and uptempo, hard country tracks such as "Thoughts of a Fool" and "Heartland."

The album reached the top of the country charts and peaked at Number Six on the pop charts. The Eric Kaz-composed single "I Cross My Heart" topped the country singles charts for two weeks. In 2003, Strait won an ACM Special Achievement Award in recognition of his 50 Number Ones. Fashions may change, but there is always room in the charts for some pure country.

Number One singles:
None

Grammy Awards: None

Label: US: MCA; UK: Universal IMS

Recorded in: N/A

Producers:
Tony Brown
George Strait
Steve Dorff

Personnel:
George Strait
Brent Mason
Brent Rowan
Buddy Eammons
Darren Smith
David Hungate
Dean Parks
Doug Livingston
Eddie Bayers
George Doering
Glen Duncan
Various other personnel

1. Heartland (2:16)
2. Baby Your Baby (2:42)
3. I Cross My Heart (3:30)
4. When Did You Stop Loving Me (2:48)
5. She Lays It All on the Line (2:30)
6. Overnight Male (2:36)
7. Last in Love (3:35)
8. Thoughts of a Fool (2:12)
9. King of Broken Hearts (3:08)
10. Where the Sidewalk Ends (3:08)
11. Heartland (Main Title Sequence) (2:42)

Total album length: 44 minutes

George Strait

GEORGE STRAIT

PURE
COUNTRY

MCAD-10651

DDD

ORIGINAL MOTION PICTURE SOUNDTRACK

Sleeve artwork by Chris Ferrara

Sixteen Stone

| • **Album sales:** 6,300,000 | • **Release date:** December 1994 |

A rare case of a British band whose US success eclipsed their domestic impact, Bush managed to sign an American record label deal without even having a UK deal in place. Strong US sales of *Sixteen Stone* eventually helped Bush acquire a British contract, if not comparable success.

Predominantly written by frontman Gavin Rossdale, *Sixteen Stone* explores universal issues such as sex, death, and religion, as well as home-grown concerns like the bombing of a London pub in "Bomb." However, it was the group's cleaned-up, Nirvana-inspired, grunge sound that the US audience really tuned into.

Ironically for such a US-styled band, production duties on their debut album were performed by the partnership of Clive Langer and Alan Winstanley. The pair had made their name producing such British musical icons as Madness, Elvis Costello, and Lloyd Cole and the Commotions. *Sixteen Stone* was released to generally negative reviews, but the video for the single "Everything Zen" became an MTV favorite and helped the album achieve gold status.

The second single, "Little Things," made Number Four on the *Billboard* Modern Rock Chart, while subsequent singles, "Comedown" and "Glycerine," both reached Number One.

Number One singles:
US: "Comedown";
"Glycerine"

Grammy Awards: None

Label: US: Trauma;
UK: Atlantic

Recorded in:
Woodstock, USA

Personnel:
Gavin Rossdale
Nigel Pulsford
Dave Parsons
Robin Goodridge
Jasmine Lewis
Alessandro Vittorio Tateo Winston
Gavin Wright
Carolina Dale
Vincas Bundza

Producers:
Clive Langer
Alan Winstanley
Gavin Rossdale
Nigel Pulsford
Dave Parsons
Robin Goodridge

1. **Everything Zen** (4:38)
2. **Swim** (4:55)
3. **Bomb** (3:22)
4. **Little Things** (4:24)
5. **Comedown** (5:26)
6. **Body** (5:42)
7. **Machinehead** (4:16)
8. **Testosterone** (4:19)
9. **Monkey** (4:00)
10. **Glycerine** (4:26)
11. **Alien** (6:34)
12. **X-Girlfriend** (0:45)

Total album length: 53 minutes

Bush

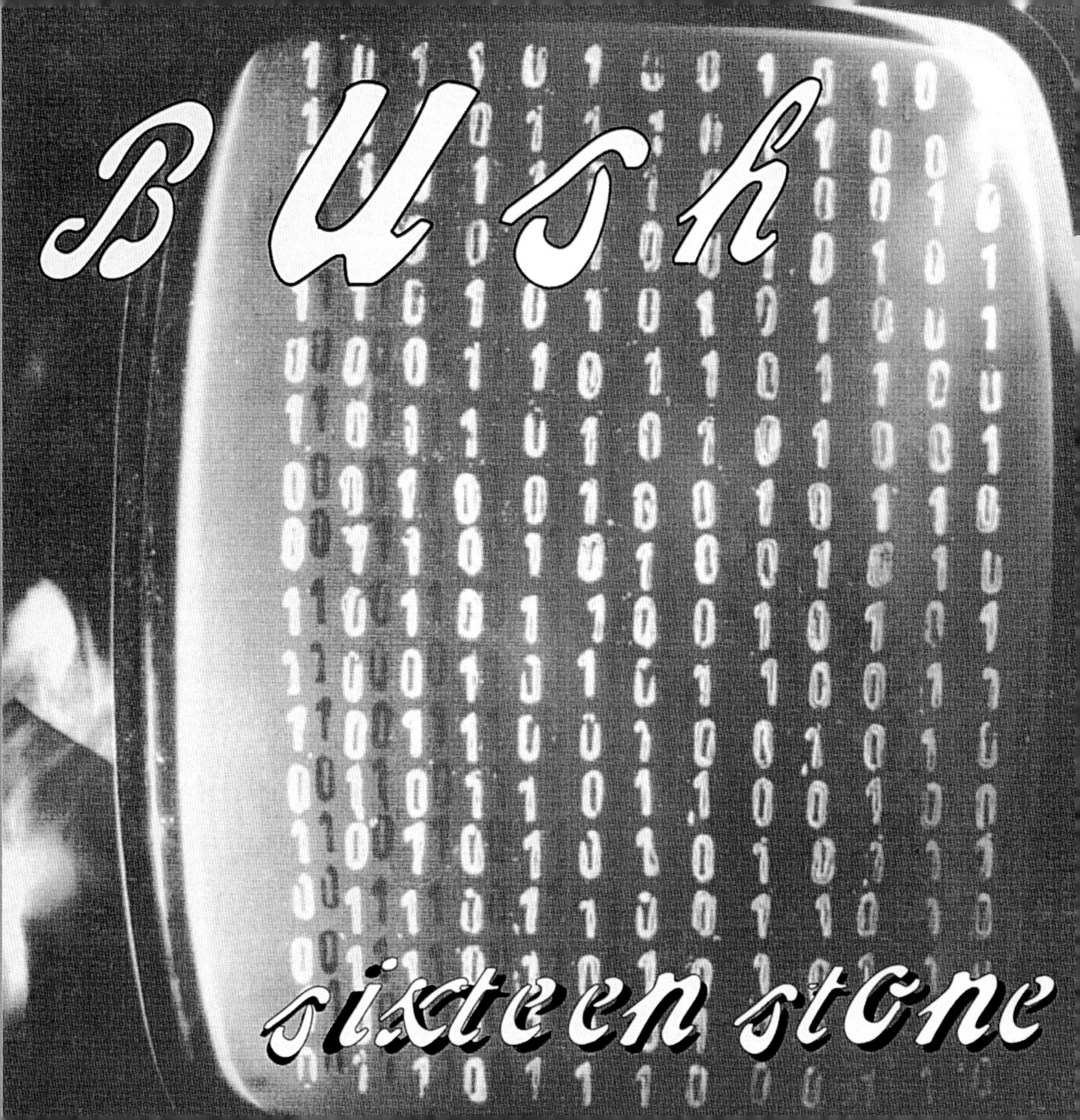
Bush
sixteen stone

Under the Table and Dreaming

| • **Album sales:** 6,300,000 | • **Release date:** September 1994 |

Hailing from Virginia and, some would argue, filling the void left in the wake of groups like the Grateful Dead and the Allman Brothers Band, Dave Matthews Band rose quickly to attention following their formation in 1990.

A heady and eclectic mix of jazz, world music, folk, and rock sounds drawn from an unconventional range of instruments, together with a busy touring schedule, saw the major labels bidding against one another to sign the band. Eventually RCA won the deal, offering greater flexibility than the other labels. The formalities out of the way, Dave Matthews Band followed their self-released live debut with *Under the Table and Dreaming*. Matthews dedicated the album to his sister, who had been murdered in his native South Africa.

The second track, "What Would You Say," became the band's first hit single, gaining airplay across rock and pop radio, as well as on MTV. Other singles, "Ants Marching" and "Satellite," would become huge live favorites.

Another busy touring schedule helped the album achieve Number Two on the *Billboard* Top 200, and more than one million sales in less than a year. Before the follow-up album, *Crash*, was released, *Under the Table and Dreaming* was certified three times platinum.

Number One singles:
None

Grammy Awards: None

Label: US & UK: RCA

Recorded in:
Bearsville, USA

Producer:
Steve Lillywhite

Personnel:
David Matthews
Boyd Tinsley
Leroi Moore
Carter Beauford
Stefan Lessard
John Alagia
Andrew Page
Jeff Thomas
Michael McDonald
Tim Reynolds
John Popper
Steve Forman

1. **The Best of What's Around** (4:17)
2. **What Would You Say** (3:42)
3. **Satellite** (4:51)
4. **Rhyme & Reason** (5:15)
5. **Typical Situation** (5:59)
6. **Dancing Nancies** (6:05)
7. **Ants Marching** (4:31)
8. Lover Lay Down (5:37)
9. Jimi Thing (5:57
10. Warehouse (7:06)
11. Pay For What You Get (4:32)
12. #34 (5:00)

Total album length: 63 minutes